The Essential Luther

North Carolina Wesleyan College

WISDOM AND COURAGE THROUGH CHRISTIAN EDUCATION

1956

ROCKY MOUNT, N.C.

The Essential Luther

A Reader on Scripture, Redemption, and Society

MARTIN LUTHER

Edited by
JERRY K. ROBBINS

BAKER BOOK HOUSE
Grand Rapids, Michigan 49516

Printed in the United States of America

Library of Congress Cataloging-in-Publication Data

Luther, Martin, 1483–1546.
    [Selections. English. 1991]
    The essential Luther : a reader on scripture, redemption, and
society / Martin Luther ; edited by Jerry K. Robbins.
        p.   cm.
     Includes bibliographical references.
     ISBN 0-8010-7759-1
     1. Theology. 2. Christian life. I. Robbins, Jerry K.
II. Title.
BR331.E5 1991
230'.41–dc20   91-30764
                                                              CIP

Contents

Preface

It has been estimated that the amount of scholarship devoted to Luther each year exceeds the quantity of writings about Jesus Christ. This fact would have embarrassed Luther, who felt somewhat uneasy about the attention his essays and books were receiving.

On the other hand, Luther was a champion of "Christian education." It was his firm conviction that Christians should be informed and should understand what they confess to believe. This passion led him to translate and interpret the Bible and to prepare catechetical and theological materials. Of all the Christian educators in history, Luther certainly ranks among the foremost.

It is in the spirit of Luther's passion for education that this handbook has been prepared. It is intended to be a brief introduction to some of the major religious ideas of the Reformer. A Luther scholar, Harold C. Grimm, has noted that Luther enunciated three fundamental evangelical principles: justification by faith, the Bible as the sole authority for faith, and the priesthood of all believers.[1] This handbook will loosely follow that outline, considering, first, Luther's view of the Bible, second, his doctrine of redemption, and, finally, his views on the role of the Christian in society.

PART 1

The Interpretation of the Bible

At 6:00 A.M. on a warm August morning in 1513 a young professor entered a classroom at Wittenberg University carrying with him a sheaf of papers containing copious notes on the first few chapters of the Book of Psalms. Thus began one of the most prodigious and productive careers in biblical studies the world has ever known.

Although Luther is remembered primarily as an outspoken activist, thundering his way through the reform of the church, he was, first and foremost, a scholar of the Bible. As a student, he concentrated on the Bible and graduated with a degree in biblical studies. His professional life centered around the Bible. One of his greatest contributions was his German translation of the entire Bible (1534). Over one-half of his works available in the English edition of his writings are commentaries on the Bible.

The Bible was the very life-blood of Luther's being. He committed large portions of it to memory. In debate and polemical writing, Luther referred to the Bible repeatedly. It was so much a part of him that he could call it forth automatically. While Luther is famous as a theologian who could mount an impressive argument for his position, the substance of that argument was largely biblical. The popular picture of Luther may be that of a man hammering his theses to the door of the Castle Church at Wittenberg University. In truth, he was more the learned monk, spending the major portion of his time in biblical study. Popular renditions may take Luther out of the study, but it is impossible to take the study out of Luther. Luther lived and moved and had his being in the Bible.

Yet to study Luther, the Bible scholar, is no easy matter. The sheer volume of his exegetical work is overwhelming. He preached, lectured, and wrote on most of the books of the Bible. This handbook will present only a small portion of the vast corpus of his commentary—the first two chapters of his lectures on Genesis. I have chosen this material because it reflects the mature Luther (1535), and illustrates his biblical exegesis in relation to philosophy and science.

1

Lectures on Genesis

By the time Luther lectured on Genesis, he had completed his study of the other portions of the Bible and translated the entire Bible into German. The Genesis lectures are the longest of his biblical studies, comprising eight of the twenty Old Testament volumes, which in turn constitute two-thirds of his exegetical material. *Lectures on Genesis* represents Luther's most mature study of the Bible and most extensive concentration on any one book of the Bible.

Chapter One

Though there has been little light from the commentators so far, and ultimately God alone knows the meaning of this chapter, we do learn, contrary to the philosophers, that the world is not eternal

From *Luther's Works* (1:3–140) edited by Helmut T. Lehmann and Jaroslav Pelikan, copyright © 1955–76 Concordia Publishing House. Reprinted by permission from CPH.

but had a beginning. While Augustine trifles with the text and gives it a mystical allegorical meaning, Moses calls "a spade a spade," and teaches about real creatures and a visible world. "Let us confess our lack of understanding rather than distort the words." Let us turn from the philosophers to Moses as a better teacher, also relying on the Holy Spirit to guide us.

First Day (Unformed Mass, Light)

(Vss. 1–2) Though Augustine said heaven and earth pre-existed, we "journey without a guide," leaving others to their opinion and following the "plain words of the Decalogue" (Ex. 20:11), which state that God created matter at the beginning of the first day. This initial mass was unformed and surrounded by water or darkness. The Spirit that hovered over the waters was the Holy Spirit. Here is the mystery of the Trinity. "The Father creates heaven and earth out of nothing through the Son, whom Moses calls the Word."

I prefer the simple meaning that can be understood by the uneducated. For those who ask what God was doing before creation, Augustine answers that he was making hell for such meddlesome questioners. The Arians are wrong in saying that the angels and Son of God were created before the beginning. We can't know God before creation because he is known only through a covering and never directly. Arius errs because he tries to do his thinking without the Word.

(Vss. 3, 5) God creates light by speaking, i.e., through the Word. This Word is God yet a person distinct from God the Father. The Gospel of John adds that Christ is with the Father from eternity, and through him, the wisdom and the Word of God, the Father made everything. As for the details, we should avoid "toying with ill-timed allegories," and should not "without reason depart from the rules of language," or "by force read meanings into words."

Second Day (Heaven)

(Vs. 6) God creates heaven out of a warm moist mist. I cannot understand Moses' division into a firmament with waters above and below, but I "take my reason captive and subscribe to the Word even though I do not understand it." The philosophers describe four elements—fire, air, water, earth—from the highest to the lowest. Though these ideas are not certain "they are useful for teaching because they are the result of plausible reasoning and contain the foundation for the arts. Therefore it would be boorish to pay no attention to them or to regard them with contempt, especially since in some respects they are in agreement with experience." They are valuable as first principles so long as we remember that God can alter the rules he has established.

Nor should we sneer at the mathematicians and their proposal of eight spheres. Theology adds two spheres but I commend Jerome who maintains silence. Rather than follow childish ideas, I confess I don't understand Moses. Aristotle and Averroes make suggestions, but "we follow Moses and declare that all these phenomena occur and are governed simply by the Word of God." We Christians must "pay attention to the expression of Holy Scripture and abide by the words of the Holy Spirit." Even though astronomy has many superstitious elements, we should not completely disregard it as Augustine did.

Third Day (Land, Water, Plants, Trees)

(Vss. 9–10) We might suggest that this belongs to the work of the second day, but God is master of his order. The land and light make the earth habitable and hold back the sea just as God saved Israel. The philosophers tell us that earth is the center and cannot fall, but they do not know that "this permanence is entirely the result of the power of the Word of God." This wonderful house to dwell in is prepared by a God who cares about us.

Herbs and trees are created in full bloom by the Word of God, though God now works through seeds. Fruitless trees and thorns came after Adam's sin. Some suggest that this work fits the sixth day better than the third, but I believe we should not view this "on the basis of our judgment." Rather than be too inquisitive, I prefer that we reflect on God's goodness in providing such an attractive house to live in.

Fourth Day (Sun, Moon, Stars)

(Vs. 14) This light perfected the sun and moon. I do not deny the astronomer's claim that the moon and stars derive their light from the sun, but I add that such power has been given to the sun by God. Augustine sees an allegory about the church, but the astronomers are the experts. It is enough that we recognize the goodness of God. We learn from reason, but theology is more certain.

The sun and moon rule as overseers of day and night. Eclipses and falling stars are signs of God's wrath or some misfortune. I have no objection to the predictions of the astronomers. "Geniuses must be allowed their pastime!" But astrology should not be numbered among the sciences because it is entirely without proof, or, at best, offers only partial proof. Knowledge of the heavens is a suggestion of eternal life. In his mind, and with the help of the mathematical disciplines, man can soar high above the earth.

I reject Plato's claim that stars and heavenly bodies include life and reason, and hold to "the Word of God and to Holy Scripture, which plainly teaches that God created all these things" that man might have a house in the future. An important principle is to "accustom oneself to the Holy Spirit's way of expression." As all the sciences have their languages and none should stand in the way of the other, so we should be able to speak of both "heaven" and "spheres."

Fifth Day (Fish, Birds, Etc.)

(Vs. 20) God can bring birds from water because the Word makes all things possible. Through the "divine rule of language . . . those things that are impossible become very easy." This strengthens faith for it assures us that God can protect us in this life and raise us to eternal life.

(Vss. 21–22) The large sea creatures are mentioned so that we not be afraid of them. All things are a praise to God's workmanship. If a species would perish, God would replace it. Procreation is explained by the philosophers but I prefer to say it rests in God's blessing and command to multiply.

Sixth Day (Animals, Man, Woman)

(Vss. 24, 26) In creating man, God summons a council and creates by a special plan and providence. Here is the mystery of the Trinity. Augustine says the image of God in man was memory, mind, and will, but I say it was existence with pure and excellent qualities of mind, spirit, and body. Erased after the fall, the image is restored by the gospel.

(Vss. 27–31) Man is created superior to the animals and with a better future. The animals are the footprints of God while man alone is his image. Eve shares dominion with Adam. Against Hilary, this detail establishes the fact that creation took place over six days. The begetting of children is a noble thing. All the good things of creation have been lost through sin.

Chapter Two

(Vss. 1–3) While God ceased creating, he did not give up preserving and governing. The rainbow, serpent, and thorns entered after the fall. If you distinguish the times, the Bible makes sense. The seventh day is set aside for worship and is a foretaste of eternal life. Moses now gives a clearer description of the first chapter, continuing his account in a connected manner.

(Vss. 4–7) The sending of rain refers to the third day and the creation of man to the sixth. Man is unique in being created from the earth. Reason is offended but it knows nothing of God. Human pro-creation today takes nothing away from the glory of man's original creation by God. The creation of man in the image of God is an allegory or dim intima-tion of the incarnation.

(Vss. 8–9) We should not worry over the location of Eden as Origen did. It is an idle question over something no longer in existence. Moses reports an actual historical place. Origen's allegorical interpre-tation is "twaddle . . . unworthy of theologians." The trees in the account are "historical facts." The fathers were led astray by allegories. After providing government, home, dominion over the animals, and a tree of life to safeguard his physical being, God provides a temple (tree of knowledge of good and evil) that man might worship him. It is an actual tree in a special grove.

(Vss. 10–18) Moses describes the garden at great length. Into this garden, God places man. Had Adam remained innocent, work would have been a delight, the garden altogether pleasant, and all peo-ple would have gathered to worship at the tree of good and evil. We must be wary of those who cor-rupt doctrine and quote partial texts. In desiring to create a helpmeet for man, God sets up the house-hold. What follows is a repetition to make it easier for Moses to describe the creation of woman.

(Vss. 19–25) Moses is still talking about the sixth day and develops more fully his earlier description of man. Though the holy fathers were great men, they erred and we do not give up Scripture on their account. They "abandon the historical account, pursuing allegories and fabricating I don't know what speculations." With Aristotle, we defend truth rather than be too devoted to friends and relatives. The creation of woman seems like a fairy tale. But reason without the Word can only lead to many perplexing mazes. "True wisdom is in Holy Scripture and in the Word of God." What person who has seen the miracle of birth today would not believe the creation of Adam and Eve. The philosophers prattle about the rib of Adam but we say, "God said," and put an end to such debates. We understand that God "builds" Eve not by any allegory but according to the "historical and strict meaning," i.e., "the wife is called a household building because she bears and brings up the offspring." Though sin marred marriage, it is a divinely ordained and blessed institution. "Thus this chapter presents the work of the sixth day a little more clearly."

2

Luther's Principles of Biblical Interpretation

Luther's writings illustrate several exegetical principles.

The Plain Sense of Scripture

Luther believes that we should always seek the plain, historical sense of the text. In discussing the days of creation, for example, Luther rejects Augustine's allegorical method in favor of a literal reading of Moses, who "calls a spade a spade." For Luther, the Bible records actual events about real things, such as twenty-four-hour days, a real moon, and an actual place called Eden filled with real rivers and live trees. In reporting the creation of light, Moses is writing history and not allegory. God "builds" Eve out of a real rib from Adam. Adam fell at a particular time, probably at noon on the seventh day. The Bible is a straightforward account of real phenomena in a visible world.[1]

Luther rejects the medieval scholastic method of attributing four levels of meaning to the words of the Bible: the historical (literal), the allegorical (symbolic), the tropological (personal or moral), and the anagogical (eschatological or mystical):

> The letter shows us what God and our Fathers did;
> The allegory shows us where our faith is hid;
> The moral meaning gives us rules for daily life;
> The anagoge shows us where we end our strife.[2]

In place of this method, Luther favors the plain sense of the text as the Holy Spirit helps us understand it. For Luther, Scripture must have a historical basis or it is a "mockery."[3] The allegorical method allows all kinds of fanciful and subjective interpretations, when, in fact, Scripture is a clear book without any hidden meanings. There is only one meaning derived from the text (not read into the text) with the aid of the Holy Spirit: "The Holy Spirit is the simplest writer and advisor in heaven and on earth. That is why his words could have no more than the one simplest meaning which we call the written one, or the literal meaning of the tongue."[4] Those who wish to stray from the words of the text have the burden of defending their position with Scripture or doctrine.[5] Thus, we are to "pay attention to the expression of Holy Scripture and abide by the words of the Holy Spirit."[6]

Although Luther rejects the fourfold method of interpretation, he cannot completely exorcise it from his thinking. He frequently allegorizes and spiritualizes the text: the creation of heaven is a sign of eternal life;

the fact that we are made in the image of God is a promise of the incarnation; and the creation of woman is evidence of the establishment of the household. Most striking is Luther's style of baptizing the Old Testament, finding Christ or the church on many of its pages.[7]

Scripture Interpreting Scripture

Luther follows the principle that Scripture interprets Scripture. Luther's commentary on Genesis contains many references to other books of the Bible. For example, Luther cites Exodus in support of the claim that matter did not exist before the creation. Several texts from the Old and New Testaments support Moses' claim that God creates through the Word (Christ). Paul supports Genesis in its claim that God created all things.[8]

While focusing on the plain sense of the text, Luther also tries to stay within the orbit of Scripture when interpreting its meaning. The Bible is to be read in the spirit of its author, or in a way that lets the writings speak for themselves: "Scripture therefore is its own light. It is a grand thing when Scripture interprets itself."[9] Accordingly, Luther frequently cites complementary texts to support his reading or to explain obscure verses.

Tradition and Scripture

Luther maintains that while tradition (the ancient fathers) can be helpful, it must always be subordinate to Scripture. Luther is quite familiar with Christian writers of the past. He is particularly well read in Augustine. The first two chapters of Luther's commentary on Genesis are rich in references to this great classic Christian theologian, as well as several others. Yet Luther is not a slave to past Christian authors, and refutes them whenever he feels that Scripture is being neglected or misinterpreted. Thus, in reference to Genesis 1 and 2, Luther rejects Augustine's claim that the world was not created in six days but instantaneously, and chides Arius for attempting to do his thinking without the Word.[10] At certain points, Luther simply ignores the classic Christian authors to "journey without a guide."[11] With Aristotle as his mentor ("Better it is to defend the truth than to be too much devoted to those who are our friends and relatives"), Luther states that "we dare not give preference to the authority of men over that of Scripture!"[12]

Hilton Oswald, in his introduction to Luther's lectures on Romans, describes Luther's method of employing both short and long commentary on the text. In connection with the long commentary, Luther would dip into the resources available in the church:

> Here he would adduce standard *auctoritates*, that is, authoritative statements, primarily from the Scripture, but also from the fathers and the more recent teachers of the church. To the latter two he might attach a refutation of the statements adduced, a new interpretation, or praise or criticism of the way Scripture was currently being understood and applied to life.

As far as commentaries, Luther

> may quote them without acknowledgement . . . or he may elucidate them with references to authority of his

own choosing, especially the Scriptures but also Augustine, Ambrose, Jerome, Bernard, Lombard, Scotus, Lyra, Occam, Biel, Faber, Reuclin, Erasmus. In any case, the utterances of men he may at any time take as materials to be criticized and refuted on the way to articulating his own Biblical stance.[13]

In sum, while Luther includes the opinions of others along with analysis of the text, such opinions are used only to illuminate—and never to substantiate— the text. Scripture is the final arbiter in all matters.

Philosophy, Science, and Scripture

Luther believes that we should acknowledge philosophy (reason) and science (experience), but only where they can clarify and support Scripture. Luther frequently cites the ancient philosophers to support his position. He is also quite open to science. Thus, in his discussion of the creation of the heavens, he acknowledges the help of philosophy, mathematics, and astronomy. The philosophers provide worthwhile knowledge in stating that the earth is the center of the entire creation and cannot fall. The astronomers correctly claim that the moon and stars get their light from the sun. While the Christian is to become familiar with the way the Holy Spirit thinks, the believer will also allow the sciences their own languages.[14]

Yet Luther does not accept astrology as a science because it can offer no proof for its claims. He criticizes careless scholarship—faulty reasoning through the use of partial data and equivocation—and calls on the services of logic and dialectic in important discussions. He debates with the philosophers on their own terms. (It should be noted, however, that Luther also held scientific notions that are now known to be erroneous.[15])

Luther, however, always "takes his reason captive" when the authority of Scripture is at stake.[16] Indeed, for Luther all thinking about spiritual things should be done within the context of the Word, or the inevitable result will be foolish conclusions.[17] Further, where reason simply cannot understand (e.g., the creation of woman from Adam's rib), Luther opts for Scripture, for "true wisdom is in Holy Scripture and in the Word of God."[18]

As an academician, Luther maintains a healthy respect for good scholarship. He also realizes that believers cannot serve God and mammon, so that the overall caste of their work, and their particular stand, must always favor religious convictions.

The Authority of Scripture

The principle that Scripture authenticates itself is assumed in all other principles. For Luther, the most important thing about Scripture is that it derives its authority from itself rather than from any external source such as tradition or experience: "This queen [the Scripture] must rule and everyone must obey, and be subject to her. The pope, Luther, Augustine, Paul, an angel from heaven—these should not be masters, judges, or arbiters but only witnesses, disciples, and confessors of Scripture."[19]

Scripture is its own authority because it contains within itself the Word or Christ or the gospel or the message of justification by faith on account of Christ. Luther uses these terms almost interchangeably. The Word is the speech and the deeds of God in creation and redemption. This Word is also Jesus Christ through whom God spoke and acted for our redemption in a most clear and effective manner.[20] By acting in Christ, God declared the gospel or the good news of salvation. This gospel is announced in preaching and is found in the Bible. The gospel is nothing other than

> the preaching about Christ, Son of God and of David, true God and man, who by his death and resurrection has overcome for us the sin, death, and hell of all men who believe in him. Thus the gospel can be either a brief or a lengthy message; one person can write of it briefly, another at length. He writes of it at length, who writes about many words and works of Christ, as do the four evangelists. He writes of it briefly, however, who does not tell of Christ's works, but indicates briefly how by his death and resurrection he has overcome sin, death, and hell for those who believe in him, as do St. Peter and St. Paul.[21]

This emphasis on the self-authenticating power of Scripture by virtue of its gospel message leads to three important implications for reading the Bible.

First, Christ is the center of the Bible and the key that unlocks its meaning: "For this much is beyond question, that all the Scriptures point to Christ alone."[22] Christ is the common theme of the whole symphony, the continuous thread that weaves through the whole tapestry. Christ is also the only meaning, the sole content, of the Bible. If Christ cannot be found in the Bible, then it is an empty book. Further, Christ is the clue to understanding the Bible, the interpretive principle that guides the reader through its mysteries to its meaning: "If you would interpret well and confidently, set Christ before you, for he is the man to whom it all applies, every bit of it."[23]

Second, all the books of the Bible are to be evaluated in terms of Christ. Luther understands the Bible as a unity of more or less important parts. He places great emphasis on the Old Testament. The Old Testament not only has great value in and of itself, but is "the ground and proof of the New Testament."[24] Further, the New Testament unlocks the Old Testament. In the first two chapters of Genesis, for example, Luther finds references to the Trinity and to Christ, and notes that certain points implicit in the text are later clarified in the New Testament. His later judgment on Genesis is that it is an "exceedingly evangelical book."[25]

Luther orders not only the Old and New Testaments but the books of the New Testament as well. The books are more or less valuable according to how well they convey or present Christ. Luther regards the Gospel of John, Paul's letters (especially Romans), and the First Epistle of Peter as the "true kernel and marrow of all the books."[26] He also highly regards the First Epistle of John, Galatians, and Ephesians. On the other hand, James is "an epistle of straw."[27]

Finally, for Luther, the gospel in Scripture is more important than the Scripture itself. The text is the final arbiter, but only because it is the voice of the gospel. The words of the Bible do not establish the Word, but the Word establishes the words. The canon does not establish Christ but Christ establishes the canon. Christ is the "Lord over Scripture."[28] As in the body, Christ is the head and the passages of the Bible are his members. Those who would read the Bible correctly pay homage to the head, unlike others who worship the members: "We have the Lord, they the servants; we have the Head, they the feet or members, over which the Head necessarily dominates and takes precedence."[29]

Perhaps the best summation of Luther's reverent and Christ-centered interpretation of the Bible are these words from his pen:

> Therefore dismiss your own opinions and feelings, and think of the Scriptures as the loftiest and noblest of holy things, as the richest of mines which can never be sufficiently explored, in order that you may find that divine wisdom which God here lays before you in such simple guise as to quench all pride. Here you will find the swaddling cloths and the manger in which Christ lies, and to which the angel points the shepherds (Luke 2:12). Simple and lowly are the swaddling cloths, but dear is the treasure, Christ, who lies in them.[30]

PART 2

The Doctrine of Redemption

Anyone who wishes to read a simple systematic theology will be disappointed with the work of Luther. For one thing, the sheer volume of his work is intimidating. Beginning in 1518, Luther wrote one or two treatises a month (four hundred titles in his lifetime). Luther's writings were forged in the crucible of intense, sweeping historical events. His theology grew out of his personal struggles. There is nothing of the cool, abstract tenor of some academic ivory-tower scholarship about his work. His writings are a confession and profession of personal faith that took shape in the midst of controversy and confrontation.

At the same time, Luther's mind seems to move in exceedingly complex paths. He never considers a topic or point without seeing its opposite or complementary side. He constantly thinks in terms of pairs: God hidden, God revealed; righteous man, sinful man; law, gospel. This dialectical way of seeing things has been described as "the maddening but expected oscillation of his logic."[1]

Although Luther's theology is experimental and dialectical, there is a focus and a unity about it. As Joseph Sittler has put it,

> There is, to be sure, a sense of the term *systematic thinker* before which Luther would not qualify—which in fact he would not understand. If, that is, the connotation of system which is proper to propositional logic is made absolute, then Luther was not systematic. But we must decidedly reject any such presumption. There is a system proper to the dissection of the dead; and there is a system proper to the experience and description of the living. There is a system proper to the inorganic; and there is a system proper to an organism. A crystal has a system. But so does a living personality in the grip of a central certainty. If, then, by system one means that there is in a man's thought a central authority, a pervasive style, a way of bringing every theme and judgment and problem under the rays of the central illumination, then it must be said that history shows few men of comparable integration.[2]

For Luther, the central certainty, the central illumination holding all his thought together and giving sense to his vast writings is the Reformation battle cry, "Justification by faith." At the very heart of all that Luther has to say is his conviction that we are redeemed by the grace of God received through faith. No knowledge, merit, or works can save us. Only the gracious outpouring of God's love can accomplish our salvation.

That gracious outpouring has happened in Christ, who alone justifies us before God: "The Word of God cannot be received and cherished by any works whatever but only by faith." Through faith we know that we need Christ, who suffered and rose again for us. If we believe in him we may through this faith become new persons insofar as our sins are forgiven and we are justified by the merits of Christ alone.[3]

As the central passion of his theology, the theme of justification by faith pervades all of Luther's writings, either explicitly or implicitly. It is difficult to find any single writing that carries the full weight of that insight. In this handbook, three works will be cited, works that range over several years and several styles of Luther's writing. The first is a portion of his *Lectures on Romans*, an early work (1515) that conveys the influence of his biblical exegesis on his theological development. Luther regarded his study of Romans 1:17 as pivotal in his understanding of justification. An autobiographical note conveys the dramatic power this passage held for him. Writing of the insight that freed him from guilt and despair, he says,

At last, by the mercy of God, meditating day and night, I gave heed to the context of the words, namely, "In it the righteousness of God is revealed, as it is written, 'He who through faith is righteous shall live.'" There I began to understand that the righteousness of God is that by which the righteous lives by a gift of God, namely by faith. And this is the meaning: the righteousness of God is revealed by the gospel, namely, the passive righteousness with which merciful God justifies us by faith, as it is written, "He who through faith is righteous shall live." Here I felt that I was altogether born again and had entered paradise itself through open gates.[4]

The second selection is *The Heidelberg Disputation* of 1518. This early defense of Luther's faith provides a summary statement of ten vital and formative years of study and teaching. It is also interesting inasmuch as the disputation, at this time, came to signify not only scholarly achievement but right faith as well.[5]

The third selection is Luther's famous essay, *On Christian Liberty* (also known as *The Freedom of a Christian*), written in 1520 in the heat of controversy and setting forth the evangelical faith in a more developed form. Here Luther carefully balances two key themes in justification: faith and works. It has been described as "the most eloquent and concise statement of Luther's faith."[6] Of this essay, Luther himself said, "It contains the whole of Christian life in a brief form."[7]

3

Lectures on Romans

Following the practice of the time, Luther's lectures on Romans were comprised of notes or glosses written between the lines of the biblical text and in the margins, and commentary or scholia on selected passages prepared separately. For the sake of simplicity, both types of notes will be presented together in this summary.

Verse 1

"Paul, a servant of Jesus Christ, called to be an apostle, set apart for the Gospel of God." Paul is to be received with reverence as if he were Christ himself and not like false apostles who are thieves and not shepherds.

[Luther first describes the intent of the letter.]

The chief purpose of this letter is to magnify sin and to destroy all human wisdom and righteous-

From *Luther's Works* (25:3–9, 135–53) edited by Helmut T. Lehmann and Jaroslav Pelikan, copyright © 1955–76 Concordia Publishing House. Reprinted by permission from CPH.

ness, to bring down all those who are proud and arrogant on account of their works. We need to break down our "inner self-satisfaction." "God does not want to redeem us through our own, but through external righteousness and wisdom; not through one that comes from us and grows in us, but through one that comes to us from the outside; not through one that originates here on earth, but through one that comes from heaven. Therefore, we must be taught a righteousness that comes completely from the outside and is foreign. And therefore our own righteousness that is born in us must first be plucked up." Our exodus is not merely from faults to virtues but from virtues to the grace of Christ. "But now Christ wants our whole disposition to be so stripped down that we are not only unafraid of being embarrassed for our faults and also do not delight in the glory and vain joys of our virtues but that we do not feel called upon to glory before men even in the external righteousness which comes to us from Christ." Thus, whether in pain or in honor or dishonor, a Christian remains the same because all is secure in Christ. But to attain to this perfection "we must in all these things keep ourselves so humble as if we still had nothing of our own. We must wait for the naked mercy of God, who will reckon us righteous and wise. This God will do if we have been humble and have not anticipated God by justifying ourselves and by thinking that we are something." Some persons can give up temporal goods but few can give up righteousness or good works. Yet nobody will be saved unless this happens as Romans 9:16 states.

[Luther next turns to the letter proper.]

Paul is not writing to scold sinners but to strengthen faith in the fight against disbelief. Up to 1:16, the text contains practical teachings on how a pastor should act. A wise and faithful servant will not exceed his authority and will not elevate his own works but will do all for the profit of his people. He will be a servant of Jesus Christ. Paul confesses he is a servant as one who received his calling from God and as one who is servant to others. His calling to be an apostle places him in an office of dignity, set apart from evil and sin.

Verse 2

"Which He had promised before through His prophets in the Holy Scriptures." In order that we not receive the glory, Paul reminds us that the Gospel had been revealed beforehand in spoken and written words, according to God's plan.

This gift (the Gospel) is not given on account of our merits, but was ordained by God before we existed (as the Old Testament amply testifies). The Christian religion is no accident but the result of God's will.

Verses 3–4

"Concerning His Son, who was made for Him of the seed of David according to the flesh, and predestined the Son of God in power according to the Spirit of sanctification by the resurrection from the dead of our Lord Jesus Christ." The incarnate Son as promised and appointed, ordained or prepared is Son of God through the acceptance of His rule and the Holy Spirit which elevated him after the resurrection. "Here the door is thrown open wide for the understanding of Holy Scriptures, that is, that everything must be understood in relation to Christ, especially in the case of prophecy."

The content of the Gospel is Jesus Christ who, although he was before creation, had a beginning, lived in the flesh, emptied himself and received power and glory. He is the Son of Man declared the Son of God through the apostles and the Holy Spirit after the resurrection. In sum, the Gospel is the message concerning Christ who was humbled and exalted. Corollary: The Gospel is not only what the four evangelists have written but the Word concerning the Son of God. It is the same Gospel no matter how many books have been written.

Verse 5

"Through whom we have received grace and apostleship to bring about the obedience of faith among all the nations for the sake of His name." Having received all things through Christ, all believers are given Grace to minister to others not by being overbearing and in order to bring the Gentiles to obedience.

Verses 6–7

"Among whom are you also, the called of Jesus Christ. To all who are in Rome, the beloved of God called to be saints: Grace to you and peace from God the Father and from our Lord Jesus Christ."

Among the Gentiles obedient in faith, you are sanctified through Christ by the forgiveness of sins which removes the torment of conscience.

Verses 8–15

"First I thank my God through Jesus Christ because your faith is proclaimed in all the world. For God is my witness, whom I serve with my spirit in the Gospel of His Son, that without ceasing I mention you always in my prayers, asking that somehow by God's will I may now at last succeed in coming to you. . . . So I am eager to preach the Gospel also to you who are in Rome." I thank God, giver of all good things and Christ our Mediator because your belief in Jesus Christ (which justifies) is proclaimed. The God whom I serve is witness that I pray for you that I may visit you and impart (not for my gain) the ministry of teaching to strengthen you in our mutual faith. Too much work has prevented me from coming to bring forth fruit among you.

Verse 16

"For I am not ashamed of the Gospel, for it is the power of God for salvation to everyone who has faith, to the Jew first and also to the Greek." In spite of 1 Corinthians 1:23, the Gospel is the strength of God for salvation for Gentile and Jew (also for the damnation of the faithless).

The power of God is understood "not as the power by which according to His essence He is powerful but the power by virtue of which He makes powerful and strong." Human power is cancelled by the Cross in order that God can give us his power. The things of the world must come to nothing. Those who do not believe the Gospel are not only ashamed of it but contradict it. "He who believes in the Gospel must become weak and foolish before men so that he may be strong and wise in the power and wisdom of God." As Christ emptied himself, hid his "power, wisdom, and goodness and instead put on weakness, foolishness, and hardship," so we must have all things as though we did not have them.

Verse 17

"For the righteousness of God is revealed in it from faith to faith, as it is written (Hab. 2:4): 'The righteous shall live by faith.'" A person's righteousness before God is from God and not from works—revealed to faith (Mark 16:16). "Only through complete belief in God will he be saved."

Human teachings tell us about the righteousness of man. "Only in the Gospel is the righteousness of God revealed (that is, who is and becomes righteous before God and how this takes place) by faith alone, by which the Word of God is believed, as it is written in the last chapter of Mark (16:16): 'He who believes and is baptized will be saved; but he who does not believe will be condemned.' For the righteousness of God is the cause of salvation. And here again, by the righteousness of God we must not understand the righteousness by which He is righteous in Himself but the righteousness by which we are made righteous by God. This happens through faith in the Gospel." As Augustine says, by imparting this righteousness He makes righteous people, and this "to distinguish it from the righteousness of man, which comes from works." Aristotle describes the righteousness of man following upon actions and originating in them. "But according to God, righteousness precedes works, and thus works are the result of righteousness." Otherwise, such works are "foolish and tricky and are to be compared with the antics of hucksters in the marketplace." "From faith to faith" does not mean from unformed faith to faith under the law, but "the righteousness of God is completely from faith," and in its growth it becomes only a clearer faith.

4

The Heidelberg Disputation

The disputation was a common teaching device in the medieval university setting. One person proposed a set of logically related theses or propositions and another person responded. Luther introduced weekly disputations to the University of Wittenberg. *The Heidelberg Disputation* dealt with twenty–eight theological and twelve philosophical theses drawn up by Luther in order to acquaint his Augustinian brothers with the new evangelical theology. Also incorporated in the following selection are Luther's short proofs for theological theses.

We present the following theological paradoxes so that it may become clear whether or not we faithfully interpret St. Paul and St. Augustine.

Reprinted from *Luther's Works,* copyright © Fortress Press. Used by permission of Augsburg Fortress.

Theses 1–3

As scripture shows, the law only hinders the way of righteousness. Further, if in response to God's gift of the law, man only sins, how much less can he do any good work on his own strength. Although human works appear attractive, they are likely to be mortal sins because they lack purity within.

Thesis 4

It is God's unattractive works of humbling and making us fearful that are eternal merits. The law shows us our sinfulness. "Insofar as we acknowledge and confess this, there is no form or beauty in us, but our life is hidden in God (i.e., in the bare confidence of his mercy), finding in ourselves nothing but sin, foolishness, death, and hell."

Theses 5–12

Because they appear good, the works of men are not mortal sins in the sense of crimes. But they also are not meritorious or sinless. Even the works that God does through us do not make us sinless. "If someone cuts with a rusty sword and rough hatchet, even though the worker is a good craftsman, the hatchet leaves bad, jagged, and ugly gashes. So it is when God works through us." The works of the saints would be mortal sins if not feared as such out of pious fear of God. When we trust our works and do not fear God, we honor ourselves and become self-confident. But this is wrong. Even dead works (not alive) are mortal (can kill) if there is no fear of God. Unless we fear God's judgment we cannot avoid arrogance. However, when we fear our sins are mortal, then they are only venial in the sight of God.

Theses 13–15

After the fall, the will is free to do evil only (and commit mortal sin). It can do good in a passive sense only. See John 8:34, 36 and Augustine: "Free will without grace has the power to do nothing but sin." While Peter Lombard grants original man free will (active capacity), Augustine denies it except as an original capacity.

Theses 16–18

If a person supposes he can obtain grace by his works, he adds sin to sin. But if the law shows him his sin he is ready to receive grace. This kind of speaking should not cause despair but lead to the desire for humility.

Theses 19–22

That person does not deserve to be called a theologian who looks upon the invisible things of God (virtue, godliness, wisdom, justice, goodness, etc.) as though they had happened. A theologian is one who sees the visible things of God in suffering and the cross, i.e., his human nature, weakness, and foolishness. 1 Corinthians 1:21. It is not enough to see God in his glory, for "true theology and recognition of God are in the crucified Christ." A theology of glory confuses good and evil but a theology of the cross sees clearly. "He who does not know Christ does not know God hidden in suffering. Therefore he prefers works to suffering, glory to the cross, strength to weakness, wisdom to folly, and, in general, good to evil." These enemies of the cross (Phil. 3:18) "call the good of the cross evil and the evil of a deed good," while "friends of the cross say that the cross is good and works are evil." To love works is to become increasingly blinded.

Theses 23–24

The law condemns everything not in Christ. Though the law is holy and good, man misuses it by taking credit for his works. On the other hand, he who has emptied himself through suffering knows that God works all things in him, and neither boasts in his works nor despairs if God does not work in him. It is sufficient that he be brought low by the cross, that he be born anew through death and resurrection in Christ.

Theses 25–28

The "righteousness of God is not acquired by means of acts frequently repeated, as Aristotle taught, but it is imparted by faith" (Rom. 1:17). "Not that the righteous person does nothing, but that his works do not make him righteous, rather that his righteousness creates works. For grace and faith are infused without our works. After they have been imparted the works follow." With Christ in us "we also fulfil everything through him since he was made ours through faith." While faith obtains what the law commands, Christ in us "arouses us to do good works." We are moved to imitate Christ's fulfillment of the commands of God. While the object of love causes love in humans, God loves the sinner. God's love also does not benefit God, but bestows good, and does not find love but confers it.

5

The Freedom of a Christian

In 1520, Luther published three major tracts setting forth the main points of his theology. One of those tracts, *The Freedom of a Christian*, was among Luther's final efforts to avoid a breach with Rome. It outlines, in brief form, many of the tenets of evangelical faith.

Two propositions guide reflection on the freedom and bondage of the spirit: (1) A Christian is a perfectly free lord of all, subject to none; (2) A Christian is a perfectly dutiful servant of all, subject to all.

Let us consider the more obvious fact that man has a two-fold nature, a spiritual one and a bodily one, an inner nature and an outer nature. And let us ask how the inner man becomes a righteous, free, and pious Christian. To become such a Christian, nothing external can help, but only "the most holy Word of God, the gospel of Christ." This alone can "feed the soul, make it righteous, set it free, and save it, provided it believes the preaching. Faith alone is the saving and efficacious use of the Word of God."

"The Word of God cannot be received and cherished by any works whatever but only by faith. Therefore it is clear that, as the soul needs only the Word of God for its life and righteousness, so it is justified by faith alone and not any works; for if it could be justified by anything else, it would not need the Word, and consequently it would not need faith." By revealing human sinfulness and the need for Christ, this faith shows the utter uselessness of works. Through Christ your sins are forgiven and you are "justified by the merits of another, namely, of Christ alone."

Since only faith can rule in the inner man, no outward work can justify. We should lay aside confidence in works and grow in faith which is the true treasure that brings salvation. Faith fills us with so great a righteousness that we need nothing more.

To the commands of Scripture, Christ adds the promises of God. The promises of God accomplish what the law demands. If we trust the promises, we will be absorbed by them. God's tender spiritual touch will communicate all things to the soul. Faith alone lives in the soul. "Just as the heated iron glows like fire because of the union of fire with it, so the Word imparts its qualities to the soul." Having all he needs in faith, the Christian has no need for the law and is free from it.

Faith also honors God by ascribing truthfulness and righteousness to him. Therefore, God, in his turn, glorifies our righteousness. Faith also unites the soul to Christ and gains all the benefits of Christ's victory—grace, life, and salvation. If we were good works from the soles of the feet to the crown of the head we would still not be righteous. "Faith alone is the righteousness of a Christian and the fulfilling of all the commandments." Faith which dwells in the heart is the "source and substance of all our righteousness."

"Should he grow so foolish, however, as to presume to become righteous, free, saved, and a Christian by means of some good work, he would instantly lose faith and all its benefits, a foolishness aptly illustrated in the fable of the dog who runs along a stream with a piece of meat in his mouth and, deceived by the reflection of the meat in the water, opens his mouth to snap at it and so loses both the meat and the reflection."

As for the outer man, works are necessary as a firstfruits of the spirit. While discipline is necessary it does not justify. "Good works do not make a good man, but a good man does good works." A man must be righteous before he does good works. Therefore faith alone justifies. Though works make a person good or evil in the sight of men it is not so in actuality. Only faith makes a person good.

We do not reject good works for their own sake but when righteousness is sought through them. The Christian lives for others not self. Since works are not needed for salvation, the Christian can consider only the needs of the neighbor. "Here faith is

truly active through love." In liberty, the Christian
empties himself taking the form of a servant. As
God has blessed us so we do all things pleasing to
him. As Christ comes to our aid, we help our neighbor—we become a Christ to the other.

We follow custom, obey the law, and serve others
not for our own justification but out of respect for
churchly authority and community, to set an example, and as an act of love for the neighbor. Do not
seek personal profit through benevolent deeds. You
do not need it.

We neither rely on good works nor reject good
works for life in the flesh. The Christian takes a middle course between law-bound ceremonialists and
those who are simple-minded and weak in the faith.
We inveigh against laws but observe them for the
sake of the weak. Despite false estimates of works,
human nature needs them.

6

Luther's Doctrine of Redemption

Luther said, "Not reading and speculating, but living, dying, and being condemned make a real theologian."[1] Surely this was Luther's experience. His credentials for writing theology were not his academic training and office, but his personal struggles with the form and content of religious doctrine—in particular, the matter of how a person is set right with God. Luther was filled with an overwhelming dread, an oppressive anxiety regarding his standing before God. Convinced that the wrath of God was always hanging over his head, he was in constant torment and spiritual conflict. Had he been approached with the question of religious zealots today, namely, "Are you saved?" the young Luther would have shuddered and fled in a panic of fear and despair.

Out of this wrestling with an awesome, unforgiving God, Luther brought forth his greatest spiritual and theological insight. From a situation of living and dying and being condemned, Luther was transformed into a world of dying and living and being affirmed. And the catalyst in this transformation was his discovery that God justifies the sinner through Christ. God is not an angry, spiteful God, intent on destroying us, but a loving, self-giving God who intends the well-being of his creation. The effective instrument and seal of this gracious divine plan is Jesus Christ, who presents the sinner blameless before the throne of God.

The Necessity of Redemption

Our redemption by God's gracious action is necessary because there is no righteousness in our human nature. Our sinfulness is both a prerequisite and a necessary condition for divine redemption. It is because we are both by nature sinful and also because we cannot save ourselves from our sinfulness that a divinely organized rescue operation is necessary. We need to be redeemed because we are alienated from God. We are sinful in the flesh and in the spirit. We follow after the things of the world, and, worst of all, we do not believe that God loves and redeems us. Unbelief is the center and source of all sin. Pride runs a close second.[2]

The law is of absolutely no use for the correction of sin. To be sure, it can make us good in the eyes of the world, but it is of no benefit against unbelief and arrogance. Indeed, insofar as the law leads us down the path of self-justifying deeds, it takes us farther and farther from God. Captive to the law, we assume we can save ourselves through our works, and, therefore, do not need God.[3]

Sin so insinuates itself into the warp and woof of the human fabric that all self-efforts at salvation fail. When we do good works to earn grace we add sin to sin. Yet we simply puff up our pride all the more, thinking that we are capable of saving ourselves.[4] There is simply no way to escape sin through our self-generated efforts. Since the fall, we can do only evil things.[5] To actively pursue good works is only to magnify our fallen nature. There is "no form or beauty in us,"[6] even when we paint our faces with piety and dress up in good deeds.

When God saves us he again does his marvelous work of creating out of nothing. We bring nothing whatsoever to the dynamic of salvation. We cannot contribute even to the *beginning* of our redemption. At the same time, once God saves us we do not become sinless. Although justified, we are, nevertheless, still sinners. Even the good works that we do are still sinful.[7]

Salvation Through Christ

We are saved by the righteousness of God imparted through Christ. Our sinfulness is displeasing to God. Sin separates the creatures from the Creator. As at the fall, so today, we alienate ourselves from God by our disobedience and shameful behavior. Descendants of Adam, we all are infected with original sin, a deep-rooted curvature inward that shuts out God and others.

God cannot overlook our sin. As it is contrary to his will, sin arouses God's wrath and calls forth divine punishment. Justice demands restitution for the offense of sin. We stand guilty before the divine court and must make payment for our offense. For reasons noted above, however, we are unable to provide payment. Because of the essential self-centered focus of all our efforts to become righteous, such efforts abort even before they can be launched.

It was Luther's genius to see that it is "the righteousness of *God*" that saves and not our righteousness. Luther discovered that God's "righteousness" does not mean his thundering judgment against sinners, but his "naked mercy" toward sinners.[8] Just as the "power of God" is a power that strengthens and empowers persons, rather than a forbidding divine attribute, so the righteousness of God is his saving action on behalf of sinners.[9] God does not so much rule in majesty from a throne as hang in humility from a cross. His righteousness is the way he lifts the fallen, restores the despairing, and recovers the lost. It is just the opposite of righteousness as a demand placed on us, a judgment leveled against us.

God's righteousness restores sinners to his fellowship through the obedient life and death of Christ. It is Christ who, by his faithful life unto death on a cross, earns the merits that we cannot achieve. Through his perfect self-giving life, epitomized on the cross, Christ satisfies the justice of God. He provides the payment that we cannot make. This action is, in turn, imputed to, or imparted to, all who believe in him. That is, there is an actual infusion or overlay of Christ's merits into or onto the life of the believer. His merits become the believer's merits, his righteousness, the believer's righteousness.[10]

The infusion of Christ's merits works justification for the sinner. By imparting his righteousness, he makes righteous people.[11] That is, although we remain sinners, God no longer sees our sinful deeds but the merits of Christ in us. God, then, pronounces us righteous "for Christ's sake." On account of Christ's merits, God's anger turns to forgiveness. The merits are like an "umbrella" protecting us from God's wrath.[12] With divine justice satisfied, we are finally restored to fellowship with God. We are "justified by the merits of another, namely, of Christ alone," and reestablished in a loving relationship with God.[13] Justification means atonement or "at-one-ment" between God and his creation, effected by God himself through Christ. All is resolved in a heavenly drama where God is both author and chief actor. Whatever else Luther said, this message of justification through the righteousness of God or the mercy of God in Christ stands among his chief insights on the dynamics of redemption.

Faith Receives the Word

It is faith that grasps the good news of justification through Christ. Justification is an action affecting the inner person or spiritual self. Since the inner person needs the Word of God to become righteous, outer works are of no use. Rather, it is faith alone that receives the Word of God; it is faith alone that justifies.[14] "Faith alone is the saving and efficacious use of the Word of God."[15] It is the way the righteousness of God for us is appropriated personally. It is the very "source and substance of all our righteousness."[16]

Since works cannot appropriate the Word of God, faith cannot be a work. If faith becomes some kind of proper attitude or necessary condition that we must achieve before we are justified, then faith is just another work shutting out the righteousness of God. If faith is a first step on the way to salvation or a "cooperation" in the process of salvation, then it is a human work and not the righteousness of God that saves us. The moment that we make faith something that we must achieve either through knowledge or action as a pre-condition for salvation, the whole structure of redemption collapses. We have once again turned to human righteousness for help and away from God's righteousness as the source of salvation. Luther puts it clearly: To elevate works "amounts to throwing the roof to the ground, upsetting the foundation, building salvation on mere water, hurling Christ from His throne completely, and putting up our own works in His place."[17]

What, then, is faith? If it is nothing, then the process of redemption is mere magic. But if it is something then it replaces the primacy of the righteousness of God in salvation. Luther tackles this problem by claiming that faith is a *passive* action.[18] It is not that we do nothing when we "have" faith, but that what we do is merely open ourselves so that the Word of God can lodge in us. Faith is hearing the Word of God announced to us. It is receiving the righteousness of God for us. It is accepting God's gracious action for us. Faith is letting God give Christ's merits to us. Indeed, faith is another way of saying Christ in us, that the Christ who is for humankind is for us in particular. Faith justifies because it is equivalent to Christ, or it is the way Christ can give himself to us.

Ultimately, faith is something God does to and for us. The very emptying of the self, the very opening of the self, is a gift of the Holy Spirit. God is at the very beginning of the dynamic of justification, preparing, guiding, facilitating. The sinner is enabled to have faith, to have the necessary passive attitude because God grants that capacity. It remains an open question, why God seems to grant this faith to some people and not to others. But the alternative to this holy mystery is to make faith into a human work and thereby end with a hopeless contradiction of logic and belief.

Luther does not puzzle over the logical implications of his view of salvation. To try to make coherent sense of it would be a failure of faith and theology. For Luther, a believer should have a "theology of the cross," rather than a "theology of glory." A theology of glory sees God in his divine works and human salvation in human works. Such a theology could boast of logical consistency. But a theology of the cross sees God in his suffering and human salvation in clinging only to Christ. This theology makes no sense as the world measures sensibleness. Here the cross is good and works are evil. Faith is living a theology of the cross, turning from power, wisdom, and glory to self-emptying and a cross. It is to become weak before others in order to become strong in the power of God. People of faith do not storm heaven with good works, but die with Christ in a baptism into his death and life. Believers have all things as though they do not have them. They count on no possession, including any goodness within themselves, to justify themselves. Their only glory is the glory of the cross, going down with Christ in a death like his, in a renouncing of all earthly securities, in order to be raised with him into a life like his, a life of trust in God and love toward others.[19]

Good Works after Justification

The story of redemption is incomplete without the presence of good works. The crucial issue is the place of works in the order of salvation. For the philosopher Aristotle, the good works that we do make us righteous. In classical moral theory, we are good according to the good behavior and good deeds that we manifest. This is not so in the Christian scheme of things. For Luther, we must first be good or righteous in order to do good works. As we are, so are our works. We must first be justified so that our deeds might be performed with the proper attitude and intent. Unless we are justified apart from works, we will do good works for our own benefit. But if we are already justified by grace, then the works we do can be turned to the benefit of our neighbor. Such works done in the freedom of the gospel can be truly acts of love and therefore truly good.[20]

Once the matter of priority is clarified, Luther cannot say enough praiseworthy things about works. Although it is an "alien righteousness" that saves us from original sin, a "proper righteousness" is needed to save us from "actual sin." Although the only corrective for an inherited curvature inward is a grace from beyond the self, the only corrective for the actual sins of daily life is an obedience to the ethical demands of the faith. It is by following the call of Christ, imitating his life in our life, that we counter the weight of the flesh and turn back the intents of a fallen will.[21]

While the inner person needs faith to hear the Word of God, the outer person needs works to give that hearing an audience.[22] Without any outward expression, faith is simply dead. "Proper righteousness" is the product and completion of "alien righteousness." It helps us to slay the flesh, serve our neighbor, and fear God, that is, to be transformed into the likeness of Christ.[23] Works follow justification as the "sign" or "fruits" of God's blessing. To the finished act of justification, works add a process of regeneration that goes on throughout the believer's life.[24]

While good works do not make us right before God they do make us righteous before our neighbor. At the same time that we are perfectly free lords of all, subject to none, we are also perfectly dutiful servants of all, subject to all.[25] In conformity to God who hides his power, and Christ who empties himself taking the form of a servant, believers become servants to others. Freedom in the gospel does not lead to haughtiness but relinquishment. God gives to us the power, wisdom, and righteousness to serve others. We should "'put on" our neighbor as though we were in the place of the neighbor. We "become a Christ" to the other, living out the servanthood of Christ in daily life. Thus, we do not live in ourselves but in Christ and in our neighbor. As God honors us with righteousness, we honor God with a faith that is truly "active through love."[26]

It is not works that we must eliminate, but false presumptions about their usefulness for salvation.[27] As soon as we are clear on that point, works flow onto the landscape of Christian life like water onto parched and barren land. They are indeed the "springs of living water," quenching the thirst, serving the needs of people weak from too little care and love. And it is the redeemed Christian who will be first in line with the healing cup of cold water.

PART 3

The Christian in Society

It has been said that everyday life was never the same after Luther.[1] Soon after Luther had set forth the major outlines of his theology in 1520, he wrote a series of treatises dealing with the role of the Christian in society. These essays were both a natural outgrowth of his insights about salvation and a response to the historical realities in which Luther found himself. Since the Christian is freed by God's grace to serve the neighbor in the world, every facet of life in the world becomes the arena of discipleship. When Luther applied this principle to actual experience it yielded specific counsel for the Christian in the realms of politics, economics, marriage, and education. So widespread was his vision that it is no exaggeration to say that through his sociopolitical writings a new light dawned on the world, forever changing the landscape of ordinary life.

The overall effect of Luther's writing was to elevate secular life to a new position of dignity and sacred importance. The medieval mind pictured a split-level world, with heaven above and earth below. Corresponding to the heavenly realm were the holy orders of bishop, priest, and nun—vocations designed to prepare the soul for salvation and eternal life. In the earthly realm were ordinary occupations essential for bodily needs and the support of the soul, but inferior to the spiritual orders. While Luther was a true son of the Middle Ages, and followed Augustine's division of reality into the city of God and the city of this world, he elevated the human order as a place where God can bless us and we can serve God.[2] Luther denied the medieval devaluation of earthly work, claiming that the jurist and baker have a spiritual value as well as those who preach and administer the sacraments. All life is the arena of God's goodness and all noble effort makes that divine goodness active and available.

Luther's baptism of ordinary life is a rich mosaic composed of many ingredients. We have already noted that the doctrine of justification contributed strong theological impetus to this baptism. Luther's early experience in the monastery and his exposure to corrupt practices in the church surely played a significant part in his rearrangement of the social hierarchy. The then current extreme efforts to empower the church with the authority of the state or to transform society into a mere arm of the church must have stimulated Luther's thinking. The necessity to instruct Christians about how to follow Jesus' ethical teachings while yet living in the world probably played into this interest. His marriage and growing appreciation of the concept of "orders" and "vocations" in society, where God's creativity and our discipleship can find expression, undoubtedly were important factors. His teaching about the priesthood of all believers is a companion theme from within the ecclesiastical structure that also fits into this whole picture.

With such a rich and multifaceted concept before us, it is difficult to find manageable selections from Luther's works that cover all the nuances of his thinking on the subject. Thoughts on the importance of everyday life and work are scattered throughout his writings.[3] Yet several works deal with the implications of his new vision for political life—in particular, the issue of authority and civil obedience. We will consider three of these writings, composed between 1523 and 1530. Although widely different in details, they share the common theme that a person can be faithful to God and neighbor in ordinary life as a subject, prince, soldier, councilman, physician, teacher, or writer. Indeed, such discipleship is not only possible but mandated.

The first writing, *Temporal Authority: To What Extent It Should Be Obeyed* (1523), sets down Luther's understanding of the role of the believer within the state. Historically, it is the first defense of temporal authority against the medieval policy of subordinating the state to the church.[4] Theologically, it provides some early glimmers of Luther's two-kingdom theory, a key concept in his thinking. For our purposes, it is important as a description of how Christians, as subjects or rulers, are to conduct themselves in the state politic. Here we have an outline of two vocations for the Christian in society.

The second and third writings illustrate several additional vocations, especially regarding responsibility to the state. For instance, in *Whether Soldiers Too Can Be Saved* (1526), we learn how a Christian can serve in the military. While there is much in this writing on Luther's views on war, our interest is in how he takes an ordinary occupation, and one sometimes thought to be as contrary to Christian principles as possible, and shows that it can be a vocation or a place where God blesses us and we can serve God. Although Christians are spiritual beings, they also have bodies and live in the real world.

The third selection, *A Sermon on Keeping Children in School* (1530), describes yet another order or estate, the realm of education. God's grace and rule are so inclusive as to include even education! God is to be found in the classroom and lecture hall as well as the confessional and sanctuary. Although some of this writing is a campaign for ministerial training, Luther gives equal space to the importance of education for law, teaching, medicine, and other professions. All professions are supports for society.

7

Temporal Authority
To What Extent It Should Be Obeyed

Although Luther earlier had affirmed the authority of the state over the church, he ignored that authority at Worms in 1521. In the midst of persecution directed against himself and his followers, Luther delivered several sermons on temporal authority in 1522. Urged by Duke John of Saxony and others, Luther in 1523 expressed his thoughts in the following treatise.

The Divine Origin of Temporal Authority

Since our rulers are taking advantage of their position by lording it over their subjects, and since this denies the divine word, it is time to set them straight. First, we must "provide a sound basis for the civil law and sword so no one will doubt that it is in the world by God's will and ordinance." Scripture well testifies to the importance of the sword to punish the wicked and protect the upright. Second, there are powerful arguments to the contrary, and these counsels to love and not return evil for evil are not meant just for the perfect but everybody. Third, there is a kingdom of God and a kingdom of the world. If all were Christian there would be no need for the law. The law is given so that non-Christians may be restrained. Fourth, there are few true Christians. "For this reason God has ordained two governments: the spiritual, by which the Holy Spirit produces Christians and righteous people under Christ; and the temporal which restrains the un-Christian and wicked so that—no thanks to them—they are obliged to keep still and to maintain an outward peace." Because there are too many non-Christians, "it is out of the question that there should be a common Christian government over the whole world." So both governments must remain and Christians must be allowed the sword when in the world. Fifth, Christians will obey authority not because they need it but for the sake of others. While the Christian doesn't need to have his or her enemy punished, the neighbor does. Sixth, if there are not enough hangmen, the Christian should volunteer because this serves the others with no personal benefit. In yourself, however, you should turn the other cheek. These two propositions are in harmony for, "at one and the same time you satisfy God's kingdom inwardly and the kingdom of the world outwardly. You suffer evil and injustice, and yet at the same time you punish evil and injustice; you do not

resist evil, and yet at the same time, you do resist it."
Suffer injustice to self but not others. Everything created by God is good including authority and subjec-
tion. Christians in particular should serve authority.
There may even be reputable vocations that Christ
himself did not pursue. Christ did not abolish the
sword. The governing authorities should help and
protect the conscientious Christian, but if they don't,
he will just have to bear the abuse. Don't go to court.
Don't swear unless needful. Since the sword is a
divine service those who wield it are in no peril provided they do not seek their own ends. To use the
sword for oneself is rarely right and only a Christian
full of the Spirit can do it.

How Far Temporal Authority Extends

It is better that the state have too little power and
punish not enough than the opposite extreme. The
temporal order should not prescribe laws for the
soul. Belief cannot be forced nor can anyone else
believe for me. Bishops should rule souls and
princes should rule castles and not vice versa. Scripture distinguishes Caesar and God, heaven and
earth. The Christian should endure any harm to
body inflicted by the state but should resist spiritual
collars imposed by the state. "A wise prince is a
mighty rare bird and an upright prince even rarer."
Force is no use against heretics since heresy is a spiritual matter. Princes and bishops put the shoe on
the wrong foot, ruling souls with iron and bodies
with letters. Princes should protect the people and

priests and bishops should serve the people rather than wield power over them.

The Manner in Which a Christian Prince Should Govern

There are three directives for the Christian prince. First, he must serve his subjects rather than himself. Following the example of Christ, he will not think of personal gain but only the advantage of his subjects. Since this may mean missing dances, hunts, and races, few princes will be interested! It is not impossible for a prince to be a Christian, but it is rare. Second, a Christian prince will respect his officials, but not trust them. Trust God in heaven but hold the reins of authority on earth. Third, deal justly with evildoers. Wink at faults and avoid war. Don't use a greater wrong to correct a lesser wrong. A prince should not go to war against his overlord. If the antagonist is equal, inferior, or a foreign government, first offer justice and peace, and, if he refuses, then use force to defend against force. Do not consider your personal interests but service to others. It is both Christian and an act of love to use force in war. If a prince is wrong his subjects should not follow him, but if it is uncertain then his subjects should obey. In sum, a prince does his job well when he prays to God, serves his subjects, is cautious with his officials, and punishes evildoers. But a cross will rest on the shoulders of such a dedicated prince.

8

Whether Soldiers Too Can Be Saved

Soon after the tragic Peasants' War of 1525, Germany was threatened with a religious war within its borders and an attack by the Turks beyond its borders. Some people were saying that Christians ought not bear arms under any circumstances. With such ferment and controversy at hand, several soldiers asked Luther for guidance, and shortly thereafter, in 1526, he issued this treatise.

I write to you who would like to go to war and yet not lose God's favor. Remember to distinguish between the occupation and the person who holds it. An occupation (soldiering) can be good in itself, but evil if done by the wrong person or improperly.

It is good for the Christian to bear the sword, but evil if the sword-bearer is evil.

Temporal government is praiseworthy. "The sword has been instituted by God to punish evil, protect the good, and preserve peace." God himself wields the sword. Yet the office of the military should not be abused. Scripture praises war and obedience rather than gives counsel to suffer and not fight. Christians live according to the spirit but also in the body. Moreover, when Christians fight, it is not for their own benefit. The office of the sword is a divine ordinance inasmuch as God has established two kinds of government, the spiritual and the worldly. The spiritual has the Word administered by preachers by which others become good. The worldly works through the sword to force persons to be good, in order to maintain peace in the world. God establishes both.

The military "is in itself a legitimate and godly calling and occupation," but what about the persons who are in it? Some people who rebel (such as those rebels who recently thought they were doing the authorities a service) do not deserve punishment. Since deeds are good or evil according to the intention we should acquit those with good intentions.

Three kinds of people make war. First, subjects war against their rulers. Only insanity, and never mere tyranny, can justify rebellion against superiors. Leave vengeance to God and pray for your rulers. Even a wicked tyrant is better than a civil war. Each of us has enough sin without adding more. Second, equals fight against equals. We should never start a war, but enter one only for protection or in self-defense or because the neighbor requires it. Christians shouldn't fight, but in their role as princes they must protect their people. If forced into war, the Christian should fear God, trusting only in Him and not the justice of his own cause. Third, overlords use violence against their subjects. Rulers can put down rebellious subjects but only in the fear of the Lord and with no claim to be right. It may be right for subjects to suffer, but human judgment cannot decide this. Rulers have no authority over superiors (God!), but only their subjects.

Several questions have been asked that need to be answered. On the issue of whether or not it is right to hire oneself out as a mercenary, I say some subjects are obligated to protect their prince and others who choose to fight should be paid. However, it is wrong if a soldier seeks gain, or is greedy for profit through his work as a mercenary. That would be to take a good work and use it unjustly. On the question of going to war for a prince who is wrong, I say obey God rather than men and do not go. On serving and being paid by more than one lord, my advice is that while a soldier's skill is worth pay, greed in a soldier is wrong. Serve the lord who is right, not the one who promises more favors. As for people who go to war for wealth or fame, they are wrong. We exhort soldiers not because of spoils to be won but because they perform a service. They should follow a king who is right or one whom they don't know to be wrong, in which latter ambiguous case they serve God. Soldiers should carry faith into battle and not superstitions. At the beginning of battle, soldiers should commend themselves to God and pray for faith whether they live or die.

9

A Sermon on Keeping Children in School

In Luther's time, training for the trades was favored over formal education. Only those persons going into professions such as law, medicine, or theology were expected to bother with schooling. Added to this, certain forces and themes in the Reformation disparaged church teachings and favored life in the spirit and untutored lay leadership. In 1524, Luther wrote a treatise that praised the schools and placed responsibility for their maintenance on the shoulders of the city managers. This treatise was largely ineffective, so Luther again addressed the issue in this sermon given in 1530.

Introduction

All preachers should urge attendance at school. We need education for ministry and government and not just for reading and arithmetic. Both God and honor require education. The devil deludes people into taking their children out of school, but without education, Germany will be "a pigsty and mob of wild beasts." Our duty as pastors is to "advise, exhort, admonish, and nag with all our power and diligence and care" so that the devil will not win.

Sermon

Part One is "a brief and cursory account of the spiritual gains and losses which accrue from the maintenance and neglect of the schools." The spiritual estate or office of word and sacraments is from God. "It includes the work of pastors, teachers, preachers, lectors, priests (whom men call chaplains), sacristans, schoolmasters, and whatever other work belongs to these offices and persons." It is up to us to honor this estate and to educate persons for it. Parents have a responsibility to see to the education of their children. There is no better work than to be a Christian pastor, preacher, or schoolmaster who can serve spiritual and temporal needs. Just think, your son could be such a person, if you are willing to provide for it. What a loss if parents fail in this, especially with boys of talent and ability. Even if a person takes up a trade later, formal education is worthwhile because it makes one a better family person and an available pastor if needed. Yes, there is a risk your son will become a heretic or knave, but that is possible in any occupation. Don't worry, your son will earn a respectable living, so long as he does not seek great wealth.

"The second part will deal with the temporal or worldly gains and losses." As an image or shadow of the lordship of Christ, the temporal office is not as noble as the spiritual estate. "Nevertheless, worldly government is a glorious ordinance and splendid gift of God, who has instituted and established it and will have it maintained as something men cannot do without." It is the source of protection for all of man's possessions. Neither beasts nor human force can maintain temporal authority but wisdom alone.

Learned men such as jurists and scholars are needed. "A pious jurist and true scholar can be called, in the worldly kingdom of the emperor, a prophet, priest, angel, and savior." You should thank and honor God if your son does this. We need schools for the office of preaching as well. At the least, there is pure pleasure in studying for one can read and travel and can live without fear of poverty. In order that we all do not become Turks, and while education is abundant and cheap and jobs are available, we should act now. "Every occupation has its own honor before God." "All the estates and works of God are to be praised as highly as they can be, and none despised in favor of another."

Even the work of a writer is honorable. It involves the best part of the body, the head. "God is a wonderful lord. His business is to take beggars and make them into lords, even as he makes all things out of nothing." So "you will find jurists, doctors, counselors, writers, preachers, who for the most part were poor and who have certainly all attended school, and who by means of the pen have risen to where they are lords." Nobility does not do it, but God alone. Though your son may beg for bread a while, don't listen to the miser who wants his son to make big money. We need jurists and men in medicine and the liberal arts. Next to the office of preaching, the office of schoolmaster or teacher is best. Honor the office of physician, also.

You are bound by the gospel to support education. Freely receiving the gospel, we should do all we can to support the office of preaching. As well, the duty of the temporal authority is to keep the children in school in order to maintain the offices and estates mentioned. If it can compel military service, the government should be able to compel education.

10

Luther's Sociopolitical Thought

To grasp Luther's sociopolitical thought is perhaps the most demanding task in the effort to get a handle on his teachings. It is very difficult to pin Luther down, to fix his position. Just when readers think they understand, Luther will drift off in a seemingly opposite direction or one that is skewed to the main line of his thought. While this style is more balanced than a narrow trajectory, and is, in part, required by the complexity of the issues and the rapid course of events in his day, it demands a daring faith and an agile mind. Among the ideas Luther asks us to juggle, let us consider four prominent themes in his reflections on the Christian in society.

God's Presence in Ordinary Life

Luther insists that ordinary life is an arena in which God is present and active. In his early theological reflection, Luther had little good to say about the world. Inheriting a dualism that placed spirit in sharp distinction from body, the kingdom of God over against the kingdom of the world, Luther regarded the world as at best inferior to heaven and at worst an evil realm in opposition to heaven. The world is full of demons, temptations, and futile strivings while heaven is the place of eternal goodness, meaning, and peace. In order to keep this world under control, God has given his law and the temporal authority. Without these correctives, the world would soon go to the dogs.[1]

Luther later modified this view, attributing some goodness to the world. This is one of the themes of his commentary on Genesis, in which he documents the original perfection of all things. He also sounds this note in his development of the notion of the two kingdoms.[2] God works not only through the sacred realm of the church but also through the kingdom of the world.[3]

God's right hand, or hand of salvation, is also the hand by which God creates and preserves all things. As well, God's left hand is God's "rule or freely given grace which is common to all," and "the bestowal of life."[4] Thus, while God raises the world to heaven in his right hand, he cradles the world, the whole world, in both hands. Or, to change the image, all things bear the signature of both his left and right hands.

Luther's elevation of the secular world finds its most developed statement in his notion of "orders." The world is the arena of God's deep and abiding creative-sustaining power. Contrary to the notions that God is an absentee landlord and the world a cosmic orphan, Luther insists that God is the very constitution of the world and the world the very offspring of God. One way this intimate interrelationship is expressed is through the fact that God has created and continues to provide "orders," or social structures such as marriage, government, and education, in which people live and through which they maintain peace, justice, and prosperity.[5]

The orders depend absolutely on God, who created them and continues to maintain them. Persons are created for placement in the orders solely by God. God makes out of nothing, that is, mere beggars and knaves, people who become lawyers, educators, and preachers.[6] On the other hand, God does not depend on the orders to make his intention known in the world. The orders are "masks" or "veils" of God's presence. God works through them, but they are "cloaks" or "covers" of his activity.[7] He is not fully revealed in the orders. Only in Jesus Christ is the believer saved. The orders, on the other hand, are wrapped up with the world and infected with sin. Life in the orders can be full of drudgery and difficulty. For instance, good leaders, administrators, and citizens are hard to find.[8] Thus, the wise ruler will realistically acknowledge the limitations of finite human nature and exercise caution in his rule.[9]

Even though the secular realm is inferior in terms of spiritual benefits and is riddled with sin, it is a vitally important, and positively significant, arena of God's activity.[10] As products of God's creative power, the orders are good. God creates all things good, even temporal authority.[11] Through the orders, God expresses his ongoing beneficent creative influence. As he sends rain for the crops, so he showers blessings on his world through the social orders. Through the rule of good government, people are enabled to live peaceful and productive lives.[12] Through the support of education, society is supplied with capable leaders for ecclesiastical and civil office.[13] The various professions in the orders are the way God's good will for his creation is manifested. The prince carries out God's intent for stable and just relationships between people. The jurist maintains order on behalf of God. Even the soldier wields the sword for God in punishing evildoers and protecting the righteous.[14] Through these various ordinary offices in the world, God is present to effect his benevolent will for his creation.

Service to God

Christians can and should serve God in their ordinary life in the world. As a child of the Middle Ages, Luther regards life in the spiritual realm as superior to life in the worldly realm. The gifts and blessings of the spiritual life far outweigh any of the pleasures of ordinary life. Life in the temporal realm is only a shadow of life in the spiritual order. Yet there is a legitimate and important place for Christian attention and effort in the secular realm. As God blesses humankind through the orders in the world, so persons can reciprocate through their participation in the orders. There is no need to run into the monasteries or go into "holy work" to be doing the work of God.[15]

Part of the background for this turn to discipleship in the secular world is Luther's view of justification. We no longer need to do holy works, or any works for that matter, in order to be saved. This means that human effort can be turned toward helping others rather than the self. Further, God gives the Christian the world, the law, and the neighbor as the arena where faith can become active in love. God's redeeming power frees the Christian for service and his creative power provides the location for that service. Christians, then, direct their energies to serving God through serving their neighbor in the world. They pursue the counsels of perfection in ordinary life as the religious do in their holy life.[16] The fruits of the spirit that blossom in the life of believers are translated into real nourishment to feed a hungry and thirsty world.[17]

The place where this service occurs is the ordinary occupation of the believer. While service certainly issues from the holy offices of preacher and minister, these are not the only places it can be found. A pious jurist is a "prophet, priest, angel and savior" in the worldly realm![18] Within one's own occupation it is possible to carry out a high and noble ministry. God has provided "orders," "stations," and "offices" in which the believer can serve God and neighbor. These offices range from parent and husband to maid and prince. They can be found in the whole sweep of ordinary daily life, from the home to the marketplace, from the school to the shoemaker's shop.

An otherwise good office can be occupied by an evil person.[19] Thus, the chief office of government in the state can be occupied by an evil person.[20] In such a case, the goodness in the office is minimized by the evil actions of the person occupying it. On the other hand, if a good person occupies the office, then that arrangement, in turn, works to maximize the goodness in that office. Such proper use of office is one possible meaning of vocation. Vocation is producing the most good in an office by consciously and deliberately turning it toward service to the neighbor.

Thus, Luther describes the work of a prince in terms of vocation. A prince can be good or bad according to the intention and manner of his rule. If a prince thinks only of personal gain, he misuses his office. A Christian prince will rule for the benefit of his subjects.[21] When he does this he is filling his office correctly and expressing his vocation in his work. Likewise, soldiering can be a good or bad office according to the way it is handled. A soldier ought not serve for private gain or be greedy for compensation. The proper way to serve in the military is with an attitude of humble faith, measured repentance, obedient service, and with no thought of personal gain.[22] To so serve is to fulfill one's vocation even in the difficult work of military action.

Obedience to Authorities

Serving God by faithfully occupying the orders means obediently following the divinely appointed authorities. While this point is a major theme in the writings here considered, it should now be apparent that it is only a subpoint of Luther's broader understanding of secular life, the orders, and vocation. It should also be noted that the readings cite exotic cases of civil obedience, such as serving as a hangman. Keeping in mind that Luther's teachings on this point have caused great controversy over the centuries, let us try to place this notion in its proper context.

The reason a Christian should obey the authorities is because God has established temporal government in the world in order to make it the most just and peaceful world possible. Were all people Christian there would be no need for temporal government. But since this is not the case, some form of rule is necessary to contain sin. A Christian state would not be right since so many people are not Christian.[23] Luther's next best suggestion is a state that wields the sword to protect the innocent and punish the guilty, and a state that educates for civil leadership and management. Because the state provides these essential services, the Christian is to obey and serve in its structures.

The Christian also obeys as an act of evangelical faith and love. Christians are not merely spiritual beings any more than the world is just a spiritual realm. The Christian lives in a body within the real physical world. The Christian faith grants no license to escape the world and its responsibilities. Indeed, just because a person is Christian is reason for deeper involvement in the needs of the world.[24] Freed from the burden of self-justification, a Christian can turn to serving the needs of the neighbor. One way to serve these needs is through temporal government. A properly managed government will provide safety and justice for all, and these benefits are the ways God's love can be operative in the secular world. Thus, Christians obey the authorities as an act of love toward the neighbor. They will even be hangmen or go to war or put up with a formal education in order to protect and preserve the rights of the neighbor.

There are some important qualifications in the obedience of the Christian. For instance, rebellion against the authorities is allowed in a case where the ruler is mentally incompetent. Subjects can also disobey orders to go to war if they think their ruler is morally wrong.[25] Christians obey only so long as this does not conflict with their obedience to God. When it comes to a decision between God and the authorities, the Christian is to obey God rather than men.[26] No participation in the affairs of state should cause believers to compromise religious principles. Thus, the Christian will, at times, have to disobey evil authorities, although again staying within the structure of government, which is good.

Another qualification is the fact that the obedience of a Christian will be rendered for the benefit of others and without thought of personal gain. If one is a prince, he follows the laws of the land not for any benefits to himself but for his subjects only. If one serves in the military, that service should provide no personal gain, beyond what is fair, but should constitute an act of self-giving for the welfare of the neighbor. While Christians must live out their faith in the world, that stance should never endanger faith or the progress of the soul to the next world. Believers bear in their body the tension of being in the world but not of it. Christians carry within themselves simultaneously worldly and spiritual responsibilities.

Bearing a Cross

Living out faith in secular society will involve bearing a cross. The Christian ought not follow the easy way of escape from the world by joining a holy order and living in a monastery. Rather, the Christian is to be fully involved in the responsibilities of everyday life. This responsible citizenship will, in itself, involve sacrifice. To remain faithful in one's occupation, to do well what one is called to do, will entail self-giving for the good of society. Life in the world means cooperation with the authorities and tempering self-interest in the interest of the whole society. A Christian will put up with all kinds of demands from temporal authority solely for the sake of assisting the neighbor.

Christian involvement in society adds several levels of sacrifice to this general civil commitment. Through their occupation, believers will go "the second mile," give up "cloak and coat," in helping the neighbor.[27] Believers will consciously and deliberately give of themselves for others in their role as husband, jurist, maid, or craftsman. While there is a certain amount of altruism involved naturally in all noble occupations, the Christian will seek the most service to neighbor that is possible. In short, Christians will turn their work into a "vocation." Believers will deny their own comfort to see that others are adequately provided for. They will live out the golden rule, doing to others what they wish others would do to them.[28] Thus, a truly Christian prince will give up certain pleasures of privileged position in order to better rule those under his care.[29] Indeed, a Christian prince, and all who sincerely fulfill their station, will suffer in their work far more than any religious professional.[30]

Another level of cross bearing in occupation has to do with the less desirable responsibilities laid on the Christian by temporal authority. This is perhaps the most perplexing kind of suffering the believer is called upon to endure. It is suffering under a government that one is called upon to support. It is suffering by carrying out duties such as punishment of wrongdoers and war against other nations that may conflict with the moral sensitivities of one's faith. While obedience to authorities is sanctioned by the Word (Rom. 13; 1 Pet. 2), the ethical implications of that obedience may create tension. Because God's will is love and nonresistance (Matt. 5:39–41; Rom. 12:19; 1 Pet. 3:9), the believer would rather not take up the sword. Yet Christians live in the world as well as the Spirit, and temporal authority requires such service from them.[31] Thus, Christians endure a conflict of conscience as a burden laid upon them by the nature of their citizenship in the kingdom of the world.

Yet another level of cross bearing is that of suffering unjust actions on the part of the government. To be struck across the mouth or openly robbed under pretext of the law are instances of unjust treatment that must be endured by the Christian.[32] If, in order to maintain order, a government rises up against its subjects, Christians can only bear the attack and suffer: "We have no power or defense against the government if it should set itself against us."[33] Even if a government is evil, its subjects are to bear mistreatment at its hands.[34] Most of all, Christians must never use violence under the pretense that it is justified by the gospel.[35] Force is an instrument of practical necessity that protects a people and a nation against the even greater evils of anarchy or subjugation by a foreign power. Force is never an instrument of the gospel.

The most demanding cross laid on the Christian in society has to do with self-defense. Here the picture is quite complicated. In the case of spiritual persecution, the Christian resists by such spiritual methods as confession, repentance, and prayer. For instance, Christians are to resist the heathen Turk with spiritual warfare.[36] In the case of physical abuse, which cannot harm the soul, Christians offer no physical resistance for their own sake, but only for the neighbor. (At the same time, it is no use to fight heretics with physical force.) In their own person, Christians will suffer physical attack.[37] But for the neighbor, Christians will join the authorities in enforcing justice, and will join the emperor in waging war. Also, while believers do not fear those who can kill the body, they do fear those who can destroy the spirit. Thus, if certain physical persecution might cause the loss of faith, such as persecution of evangelical believers, then this can be met with physical resistance.[38] Even with all these qualifications to a nonresistant style of life, Christians use physical force only as a last resort and with regret while confessing their sinfulness.

In sum, so far as life in the world is concerned, Christians are dual, split-level persons. On the one hand, Christians are public persons, ordinary citizens who occupy common offices and behave in the usual modes of social interaction, using force, punishment, and weapons of war. On the other hand, Christians are private persons, imaging God, harboring faith, and expressing love, and in this person they must not use force.[39] The Christian wears two hats: "So he lives simultaneously as a Christian toward everyone, personally suffering all sorts of things in the world, and as a secular person, maintaining, using, and performing all the functions required by the law of his territory or city, by civil law, and by domestic law."[40] The Christian, then, has always to decide when to suffer and when to act.[41] This may not be a particularly comfortable or even a logically unified posture, yet to opt for less would be to deny the fullness and complexity of Luther's picture of the Christian in society.

While the realms of faith and life, the sacred and the secular, the spiritual order and the worldly order are to be differentiated in certain important ways, they are not to be totally separated. This is especially the case when viewing the world we live in. This reality is yet one of God's "kingdoms." The holy pervades the secular. God's grace is a "real presence" on this earth. Just as Luther discovered that it is no longer necessary to mount up to heaven to find God, but he is there on the cross, so he argued that Christians no longer need to do "holy things" to please God, but only bear their cross for the sake of the neighbor. Christian life in society embodies that strange biblical inversion in which the way to find life is to lose it. By giving our lives for the sake of our neighbor, we become fully present to ourselves and to the world.

Notes

N.B.: Citations from Luther are taken from Helmut T. Lehmann and Jaroslav Pelikan, eds., *Luther's Works*, 55 vols. (Philadelphia: Fortress; St. Louis: Concordia, 1955–76). Hereafter it will be referred to as *LW*. The first number cited is the volume number; the following numbers are page numbers.

Preface

   1. *LW* 31, "Career of the Reformer," 1:x.

Chapter 2

   1. *LW* 1:5, 19, 40, 82, 87–88, 131–32.
   2. *LW* 1:87.
   3. *LW* 10:4 ("First Lectures on the Psalms").
   4. *LW* 39:178 ("Answer to the Hyperchristian Book").
   5. *LW* supp. vol., 126.
   6. *LW* 1:30.
   7. *LW* 1:18, 39, 87, 103.
   8. *LW* 1:6, 17, 18.

9. Paul Althaus, *The Theology of Martin Luther*, trans. Robert C. Schultz (Philadelphia: Fortress, 1966), p. 76.

10. *LW* 1:4, 14.

11. *LW* 1:6.

12. *LW* 1:122.

13. *LW* 25: x–xi (Hilton Oswald).

14. *LW* 1:26–29, 35, 41, 47.

15. *LW* 1:45, 52, 108–10, 123.

16. *LW* 1:26.

17. *LW* 1:13.

18. *LW* 1:125.

19. *LW* 26:58 ("Lectures on Galatians," hereafter, "Lectures").

20. *LW* supp. vol., chap. 3.

21. *LW* 35:360 ("Preface to the New Testament," hereafter, "New Testament").

22. *LW* 35:132 ("Avoiding the Doctrines of Men").

23. *LW* 35:247 ("Preface to the Old Testament," hereafter, "Old Testament").

24. *LW* 35:236 ("Old Testament").

25. *LW* 35:237 ("Old Testament").

26. *LW* 35:362 ("New Testament").

27. Ibid.

28. *LW* 26:295 ("Lectures").

29. *LW* 34:112 ("Theses Concerning Faith and Law").

30. *LW* 35:236 ("Old Testament").

Part 2

1. John R. Loeschen, *Wrestling with Luther: An Introduction to the Study of His Thought* (St. Louis: Concordia, 1976), p. 151.

2. *LW* supp. vol., 42–43.

3. *LW* 31:346, 347.

4. *LW* 34:337 ("Preface to Latin Writings").

5. *LW* 34:xiv.

6. J. M. Porter, *Luther: Selected Political Writings* (Philadelphia: Fortress, 1974), p. 25.
7. *LW* 31:343.

Chapter 6

1. John R. Brokhoff, *Luther Lives* (Lima, Ohio: CSS, 1983), p. 24.
2. *LW* 31:304 ("Two Kinds of Righteousness," hereafter, "Two Kinds"), 362, 47–48; 34:154–56 ("The Disputation Concerning Justification," hereafter, "Disputation").
3. *LW* 31:42–43, 54–55, 356.
4. *LW* 31:50.
5. *LW* 31:48–49.
6. *LW* 31:44.
7. *LW* 25:136–37, 150–51; 31:45.
8. *LW* 25:137.
9. *LW* 25:149, 151.
10. *LW* 31:346, 349, 351.
11. *LW* 25:151–52.
12. *LW* 34:153 ("Disputation").
13. *LW* 31:347.
14. *LW* 31:344–46.
15. *LW* 31:346.
16. *LW* 31:353.
17. *LW* 21:288 ("Sermon on the Mount").
18. *LW* 31:49–50.
19. *LW* 25:150–52; 31:52–55.
20. *LW* 25:151–52; 31:55–56, 361–62, 364–71.
21. *LW* 31:297–300 ("Two Kinds").
22. *LW* 31:358ff.
23. *LW* 31:299–300 ("Two Kinds").
24. *LW* 31:300 ("Two Kinds").
25. *LW* 31:344.
26. *LW* 31:364–68, 371.
27. *LW* 31:363, 372–73.

Part 3

1. Donald R. Heiges, *The Christian's Calling* (Philadelphia: Muhlenberg, 1958), p. 64.
2. Paul Althaus, *The Ethics of Martin Luther,* trans. Robert C. Schultz (Philadelphia: Fortress, 1972), pp. 51–53.
3. See especially Gustaf Wingren's *Luther on Vocation,* trans. Carl C. Rasmussen (Philadelphia: Muhlenberg, 1957), and George W. Forell's *Faith Active in Love: An Investigation of the Principles Underlying Luther's Social Ethics* (Minneapolis: Augsburg, 1954).
4. *LW* 45:80.

Chapter 10

1. *LW* 45:91; 46:217
2. Heinrich Bornkamm, *Luther's Doctrine of the Two Kingdoms in the Context of His Theology* (Philadelphia: Fortress, 1966), p. 8.
3. *LW* 45:91–92.
4. Paul Althaus, *The Theology of Martin Luther,* trans. Robert C. Schultz (Philadelphia: Fortress, 1966), p. 106; *LW* 10:11 ("First Lectures on the Psalms").
5. Martin J. Heinecken, "Luther and the 'Orders of Creation' in Relation to a Doctrine of Work and Vocation," *Lutheran Church Quarterly* 4 (1952): 393–414.
6. *LW* 46:250.
7. Althaus, *Theology*, p. 22.
8. *LW* 45:113.
9. *LW* 45:121–23.
10. *LW* 46:99–110, 237.
11. *LW* 45:99; 46:237–38.
12. *LW* 45:91; 46:251–52.
13. *LW* 46:228, 241.
14. *LW* 46:96.
15. *LW* 21:269 ("The Sermon on the Mount," hereafter, "Sermon").

16. *LW* 45:87–88.
17. *LW* 21:258 ("Sermon").
18. *LW* 46:240.
19. *LW* 46:94, 97, 248; 21:278–79 ("Sermon").
20. *LW* 46:115–16; 45:113.
21. *LW* 45:120.
22. *LW* 46:123–24, 129.
23. *LW* 45:91.
24. *LW* 45:100.
25. *LW* 46:130.
26. *LW* 45:125.
27. *LW* 45:96.
28. *LW* 21:235–36 ("Sermon").
29. *LW* 45:121.
30. *LW* 45:126; 21:256 ("Sermon").
31. *LW* 45:87, 89.
32. *LW* 21:114 ("Sermon").
33. *LW* 46:29, 32 ("Admonition to Peace," hereafter, "Admonition"); *LW* 21:115 ("Sermon").
34. *LW* 46:28 ("Admonition").
35. *LW* 46:50–51 ("Against the Robbing and Murdering Hordes of Peasants"), 70–71 ("An Open Letter on the Harsh Book Against the Peasants").
36. *LW* 46:170–72 ("On War Against the Turk").
37. LW 46:29, 32, 35 ("Admonition").
38. *LW* 47:19 ("Dr. Martin Luther's Warning Against His Dear German People").
39. Althaus, *Ethics*, pp. 66–69.
40. *LW* 21:113 ("Sermon").
41. Bornkamm, *Luther's Doctrine,* p. 23.